THE LITTLE

YORKSHIRE
PROVERBS

compiled by Peter Lindup

Dalesman

First published in Great Britain 2009 by Dalesman Publishing
an imprint of
Country Publications Ltd
The Water Mill, Broughton Hall
Skipton, North Yorkshire BD23 3AG

Reprinted 2015

ISBN 978-1-85568-270-2

Printed in China on behalf of Latitude Press Ltd.

Introduction

"You can tell a Yorkshireman but you can't tell him much", goes the saying, and this collection of humorous and enlightening proverbs and sayings, compiled from the 'Old Amos' column in *Dalesman* magazine, proves that Yorkshire folk always have a ready comment or astute insight on all aspects of life, and is full of traditional and down-to-earth Yorkshire wit and wisdom.

He 'at knows nowt, doubts nowt.

A word of advice: nivver give it.

Thoo's aboot as nimmle as a
steean pig-trough.

You nivver knaw 'ow clever you are
till you've failed.

Experience is summat tha nivver
'as till just after tha needs it.

Misfortunes come baht seekin' 'em.

It's better ter enjoy t' breet days
than brood ovver t' dark uns.

"Misfortunes nivver come singly",
as t' chap said when t' midwife
told him his wife 'ad just 'ad triplets.

If thou wants ter find out who thy friends are, ask a favour on 'em.

It's a wise hiker that can enjoy
t' scenery even if he dun't
get ter t' top.

A bletherin' coo sooin
fergets 'er cawf.

He's t' sort o' person you like better
t' less you see on him.

Talk abaht hard-faced, ye could straighten nails on it.

Tek time bi t' foot whahl yer may, for ther's neea kenning when eternity'll tek yer by t' hand.

For a long life, be moderate in all things — but doan't miss aht.

Soft sooap'll grease t' stiffest 'inge.

T' trouble about doing nowt is
— yer can't tek time off.

T' hardest work of all is doin' nowt.

It's a gift that God's gi'en, fer dirty watter to wesh clean.

How do you tell young plants from weeds? Pull 'em all aht. If they come up again, they're weeds.

What tha wants for working is a
cast-iron back wi' a hinge on it.

It's t' person 'at works when there's nowt to do that gets to t' front.

Think o' marriage as an investment: it pays thee dividends, if thou pays interest.

Nivver put thi 'usband on a pedestal;
he'll nobbut want dusting.

T' world's biggest underdeveloped
territory lies under thee hat.

Go any slower an' yer'd be doin'
yisterday's work.

Opportunity knocks once
— and t' neighbours ivver after.

A bachelor is a chap who nivver maks t' same mistake once.

Thou mun mek the most o' thissen;
it's all tha's getten.

There's allus more to life than trying
ter mek it go quicker.

Dew as they dew i' Dent;
if tha's no bacca, chew bent.

A free lunch at a public hahse is
t' deearest meal o' t' day.

Folk are like tea. You can nivver judge o' their quality till they get into hot watter.

Is t' tea begrudged,
or t' watter bewitched?

Some fowk are nivver closer than
when comparing ailments.

You can't make good fooid better bi serving it i' fancy dishes.

There's nowt so queer as fowk
— specially wick uns.

There's nowt wrong wi' reight fowk.

She talks looads but says nowt.

She's a lass o' few words but she uses 'em a heck of a lot.

If there's ivver owt good,
there's nivver owt left.

He's nobbut hauf-rocked 'at believes ivverything he's told, but he's clean oot of his heead 'at believes nowt.

Bread is t' staff o' life but
Yorkshire pudding's a rare crutch.

Clogs ter clogs i' three generations.

Tha can allus tell a sensible chap
— he thinks on t' same lines
as thissen.

Some fowk nivver hide their leet
under a bushel wi'out tellin' fowk
which is t' bushel.

Strength goes in at t' mooth.

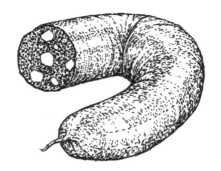

Old age is like owt else: to mek
a success on it, thou's got
to start young.

There's one thing abaht bein' poor
— it costs nowt.

It's grand to buy things 'at cost brass,
but don't lose things 'at cost nowt.

T' brass tha owes is allus more than tha reckoned, and t' brass owed to thee is allus less than tha thowt.

T' reason tha can't tek thi brass wi' thi is that it allus goes afore thee does.

Allus borrow thi neighbour's lawnmower when he tells thi his daughter's starting her piano practice.

A wise fatther'll allus bring up his
bairns i' t' way 'at 'e owt to
'a' gone hissen.

A woman's work is nivver done —
an' some dooan't seemed to
be ashamed of it nawther.

It's a forrard lass 'at casts many a
backard glance.

There's nowt good 'at's cheap.

A laugh at yer own expense
costs nowt.

Women like to be flattered;
men like to flatter thersens.

She's unheaped an' doon-thrussen
wi' wark.

Let your missus know who t' boss is reight from t' start — it's no use kiddin' thissen.

If tha's in t' reight, argify like a man;
if tha's in t' wreng, argify like a woman.

Hoss-power were a lot safer when just t' hosses 'ad it.

T' best way to travel on t' rooads is
behind a herd o' coos.

A tale efther it's been telled bi three women owt ti start frae scratch again.

Thoo gans aboot as if deead lice was droppin' off tha.

If tha can tell t' difference between good advice an' bad advice, tha doesn't need advice.

An optimist is t' chap who knows when his boots wear out 'e'll be back on his feet.

'E's that mean,
'e'd nip a curran' i' two.

Where there's muck there's brass.

Ivverything's good to good fowk.

It's better to fettle an' shout about it,
ner nivver to fettle at all.

Tha can onny understand life if tha looks at it back'ards, but tha's got to live it forrards.

From Hull, Hell and Halifax
May the good Lord deliver us,

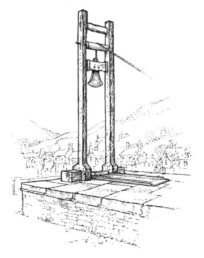

Tha can allus tell a Yorkshireman
— but not much.

.

Them 'at eyts mooast puddin' gets
mooast meat.

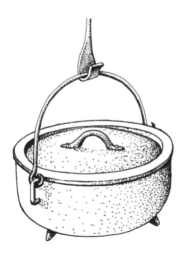

Why give up bad habits when tha feels no better for it?

Moderation's all reet as long as tha dun't ovverdo it.

Poverty wun't be half as bad ter bide
if other fowk didn't know abaht it.

Fowk who have more brass than brains usually 'aven't got a lot o' brass in t' fust place.

Some fowk are like blisters
— they only appear when
all t' work's done.

A man's nivver too tired to let fowk
know 'ow 'ard 'e's worked.

Fowks 'at think least, talk mooast.

Dull minds an' sharp tongues
allus go together.

'Is nooase leuked as if it hed bin set on 'warm'.

He's sich a throit,
a pint nobbut wets one side.

Knowin' what tha's saying is allus
better than sayin' what tha knows.

When a chap swanks about what
'e knaws, then 'e's showing
'is ignorance.

When yer all alone bi yersen,
watch yer thowts.

It's daft ter fret ovver a burnt cake afore thou's put it in t' oven.

He's like a ferret
peepin' oot of a wau-hole.

Winter-sown wheat,
and summer-proud lass,
wean't fetch t' farmer
varry much brass.

It's easy ta tawk
on a warm 'earthstun.

As throng as Throp's wife,
who brewed an' weshed an' baked
all on t' same day — an' then 'anged
'ersen wi' t' dish-claht.

Round t' wood and round t' wood,
an' a crooked stick at last.

Nivver tell a chap 'is faults. Tell 'em to 'is wife instead. She'll be reight suited, an' 'e'll get to 'ear about 'em just t' same.

Doon't fret ovver a small crisis
— there'll soon be a bigger un
to worry abaht.

Tha's mekkin' progress if each mistake tha meks is a new un.

It may be clivver ti stop a bull,
but it's wiser ti fasten t' gate
in t' fust place.

As queer as Dick's hatband,
'at went nine times rahnd
an' still wouldn't tee.

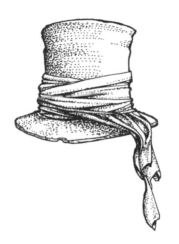

'E's that well off
'e's bow-legged wi' 'is brass.

Tha can't mak hunters
oot o' hairy-legged uns.

Nowt nivver comes ter nowt.

He wed t' midden fer t' muck,
an' gat puzzoned wi' t' stink.

Shak a bridle ovver a Yorkshireman's grave an' 'e'll gerrup an' steal t' hoss.

Thou doesn't want ti be knockin' snaw off tonnups when thoo's sixty.

'E couldn't stop a pig in a ginnel.

There's most fratchin'
wheer there's least room.

Yorkshire fowk 'll push ther way through t' Pearly Gates while other fowk stand an' staare at 'em.

Some fowks are allus leetin' on theer feet, while others hezzant a leg ta stand on.

Hitch thy wagon to a pair o' good hosses, and let t' star dew its awn job.

A pint of oil gans fother than a gallon o' vinegar, onny day.

T' same brass 'll buy awther new booits or old beer.

Noisy sorra maks noa furra,
Silent grief furras deep.

Yorkshire born and Yorkshire bred,
strong in t' arm an' thick in t' 'ead.

Yorkshire folk's 'earts are like their puddings: crisp outside, but soft within.

T' nearest some fellers ivver get to
gardening is diggin' up t' past.

As idle as Ludlam's dog
'at leaned agin t' wall ter bark.

He's allus in t' field when he should be in t' fowd.

Nine out o' ten as reach t' top
o' t' ladder have had someone
hoddin' it for 'em.

It's neea use leein' to them 'at knaws.

Doan't believe all tha sees
— fathom it.

Whativver question thoo gits axed, knaw nowt.

A Yorksherman i' Lundun is thowt
by a goood monny to be as mich use
as a bull in china shop.

Other books published by Dalesman:

The Little Book of Yorkshire Dialect

The Little Book of Yorkshire Christmas

The Little Book of Yorkshire

Yorkshire Dialect Classics

Yorkshire Dialect Dictionary

For a full list of our books, calendars, DVDs, videos and magazines, visit www.dalesman.co.uk